H   OW?

I

This book is to be returned on
or before the date stamped below

E

UNIVERSITY OF PLYMOUTH

EXMOUTH LIBRARY

Tel: (0395) 255331
This book is subject to recall if required by another reader
Books may be renewed by phone
CHARGES WILL BE MADE FOR OVERDUE BOOKS

COLLINS
EDUCATIONAL

CONTENTS

You	3
Age in disguise	7
Family	11
Memories	18
People as observers	20
Opinions	22
Bias	24
Photographic evidence	26
Summarising	30
Yesterday's news	32
Change	35
Documentary or written evidence	37
A historical detective story	42
In my time	44
A time capsule	46
Index	48

© 1986 John Cockcroft

First published in Great Britain 1986 by
Collins Educational
8 Grafton Street, London W1X 3LA

Designed by Bob Wright, cover by Pinpoint Design
Typeset by Hope Services
Printed and Bound in Great Britain by Martin's of Berwick
Reprinted twice 1987, 1988

ISBN 0 00 315401 7

You

Asking questions

This is a history book. It is a very special sort of history book, not about kings and queens, heroes and heroines, battles or inventions. It is about you. You are the main character, although other people will be mentioned. This book is about your life.

Who knows most about you? You of course are an expert. Where are you going to start? Make a list of questions that you would like to ask yourself. Questions are important in history.

Here are a few to start you off:

What is my name?
What colour is my hair?
Where do I live?
Who are my friends?
What is my favourite
television programme?

I expect most of your questions begin with 'What', 'Where' or 'Who'. Are there any beginning with 'Why'?

Look again at your list of questions and use them to ask some 'Why' questions, like these:

Why am I called by these names?
Why are these children my friends?
Why do I like this television programme?

Your list of questions should be quite long. It shows what an important *source* you are for this topic.

Making a questionnaire

Now try to arrange the questions into groups with something in common. For example, all the questions on the way you look can go in one group:

What colour is my hair?
What colour are my eyes?
How tall am I?

Kelly

What is my name?
Why is my name Kelly?
Where do I live?
Why do I live at 111 AShcroft Road
HoW old am I?
What colour are my eyes?
What is my heigt?
have I got Short hair?
Whatis my mums name?
What are my pets?
Would my mum let me be a punk?
Who is my best friend?
Why is Jackie my best friend?
Whats my Teachers name?
Why is Simon LeBon my favorite pop star?
What is my favorite T.V. programe?
Why do I cry when I am sad?
What makes me sad?
Why am I silly
What makes me happy?
Why am I kind
Why am I some times mean?
Why am I some times cross?

CHRISTOPHER CHAMBERLAIN

Why do I like Paul?
Why do I like Matthew?
Why do I like t.v?
How was I born?
Why am I called Christopher?
Why do I like football?
Why can't I skip?
Why am I tall?
Why am I brown?
Why dont I live in Australia?
Why do we play football with tennis balls?
Why have I got a computer?
Why is it cold in the winter?
Why is my mum married?
How did my mum get married?
Why do I like green?
Why do I play with George?
Why do I like cricket?
Why am I a boy?
Why do I play rounders?
Why do I have to go to bed?
Why don't I live in London?

Here are two children's questionnaires. Do not copy them. Think of questions about yourself.

All the questions on your hobbies or what you like doing can go in another group, and so on. Do not forget to leave spaces for the answers.

When your questionnaire is complete you can ask yourself the questions and fill in the replies.

Perhaps you found that some of the questions that you asked about yourself were not very easy to answer. 'Why do I live here?' might be a question like this. What can you do to find the answers? Do not forget that this part of the book is about asking questions. Make a list of people who might tell you more about yourself. My teacher, my parents, my friends, for example.

Personality

What are you like as a person? Are you bossy, shy, silly or polite, for example? Now add a few questions, and answers, to your questionnaire to help show what sort of person you are. Here are some words that you might use:

sensible	noisy	shy	lazy	impatient
miserable	unfriendly	happy	kind	mean

(It might help to find the opposites of these words.)

Do you think other people would agree with what you think about yourself? How could you find out what they think?

Would you expect everybody to think the same?

For a group

Here is an example of a special sort of questionnaire.
Who do you think uses this form? How do you know?

Make a copy of it and try filling it in with details of one person in the group. Do not use the real name. Make one up. Make up something which you could write on the form under the heading 'Current offence'.

CIRCULATION IN ALL POLICE BULLETINS
Complete a separate form for each individual

DESCRIPTION OF SUSPECT

Case No.		Officer on Case
Police Station		Date
Surname	Christian Name(s)	Sex
Alias		Nationality
Place of Birth	Age	Date of Birth
Height	Build	Hair (Colour/Style)
Colour of Eyes	Marks/Scars	Dress
Accent	Type of Personality (See List B overleaf)	
Occupation	Last Known Address	

Previous Convictions (Offences, Dates, Sentences)

CURRENT OFFENCE

Time	Date	Place

Description of Offence in Full

Now exchange forms with another group. Draw pictures of the people whom the forms describe. Can you work out who the people really are?

Age in disguise

Clues are misleading

History is a kind of detective story. Detectives always ask questions about the *evidence* or the clues that they find. The answers can be used as new clues for further investigation.

For example, you know how old you are and how tall you are, but is there a connection between the two? Is the first a clue to the second?

Here are ten children from the same class. They have been '*ranked*' according to size. That means that they have been sorted out so that a smaller one always comes before a bigger one.

Teresa   Laura   John   Clare   Tom   Jack   Jim   Fred   Sarah   Ann

Who do you think is oldest? Youngest?

Here is a list of the children's names and ages but the ages are mixed up. Can you sort out the ages and put the correct age against each child?

Teresa	10 years	2 months	Jack	9 years	11 months
Laura	10 years	7 months	Jim	10 years	6 months
John	10 years	0 months	Fred	10 years	1 month
Clare	9 years	0 months	Sarah	10 years	7 months
Tom	10 years	3 months	Ann	10 years	2 months

The connection between age and size is not a very good clue. The label inside your shirt or blouse may show the size in years. You might be wearing a shirt which is labelled '8–9 years', but that doesn't prove that you actually are that age.

'But it says for a 9–10 year old!'

The children's real ages and heights are:

Teresa	9 years	0 months	(1.28 m)	Jack	10 years	2 months	(1.40 m)
Laura	10 years	3 months	(1.30 m)	Jim	10 years	7 months	(1.42 m)
John	9 years	11 months	(1.32 m)	Fred	10 years	6 months	(1.44 m)
Clare	10 years	2 months	(1.34 m)	Sarah	10 years	1 month	(1.48 m)
Tom	10 years	7 months	(1.36 m)	Ann	10 years	0 months	(1.50 m)

Plot their ages on a graph, like this:

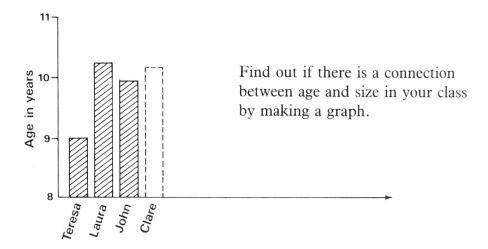

Find out if there is a connection between age and size in your class by making a graph.

You can make a further investigation by taking a few children from each class in your school. Does there seem to be any pattern? Are boys usually taller than girls of the same age, for example?

You could even try ranking your teachers in order of age. You will probably have to guess what their ages are. Do you agree in your guesses?

Clues need more evidence

It is always difficult to tell exactly how old people are. Some old people like to look younger than they really are, and some young people try to look a bit older. Some people have grey hair or wrinkles even when they are not very old.

How could you make yourself look older?

One obvious way is to wear clothes that older people often wear. A girl might use make-up to look older. You could add touches of grey to your hair to look older. But your age wouldn't have changed.

Beware: clues are often *misleading*.

1   2   3   4   5   6   7   8

Can you guess which of the descriptions below fits which of the people in the picture above? (Answer on next page)

Sister Jane is 12, weighs 42 kg and is 1.5 m tall
Aunt Anne is 39, weighs 55 kg and is 1.6 m tall
Uncle Bill is 42, weighs 95 kg and is 1.8 m tall
Cousin Karen is 25, weighs 51 kg and is 1.8 m tall
Great Aunt Molly is 77, weighs 45 kg and is 1.5 m tall
Brother Jim is 20, weighs 70 kg and is 1.9 m tall
Cousin Peter is 15, weighs 55 kg and is 1.7 m tall
Grandfather Jones is 80, weighs 83 kg and is 1.8 m tall

A fine Tudor-style country house in superb unspoiled surroundings

Many clues need more evidence to support or explain them.

Objects may be just as misleading as people. How old do you think these articles are?

In fact they are all fairly new. Some modern fashions look like old ideas. Some people like collecting copies of old things. These are called *replicas*. Some people like houses which look as if they were made with old materials, but which are really built by modern methods. Always be suspicious of clues.

Family

History is about people

When you answered your questions about yourself you may have spoken to somebody who knows you almost as well as you know yourself — perhaps even better. This was probably someone in your family. With you as the central character of this book we cannot ignore your family. It may be large or small. You may have certain jobs or responsibilities in your family. Do you wash up or help with the shopping for example?

Some members of your family are responsible for parts of your life. Who buys your clothes, for instance? When you talk to your friends, you may notice that ideas about families are not all the same. This is because there are many different types of family. These pictures show four different kinds. Is your family anything like any of these? Try to decide how the people in each picture may be related to each other. Why are the numbers in each family so different?

When you have talked about these things, turn over the page. On the back of each picture are a few details about each family.

How do these facts fit in with your own ideas about the pictures? Do they give you more or different ideas about each kind of family?

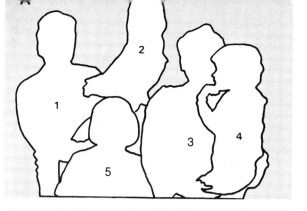

A

A nuclear family
1   Mr Nicholls
2   Daughter Deborah
3   Mrs Nicholls
4   Daughter Julia
5   Daughter Rebecca

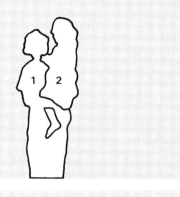

B

A single-parent family
1   Mother
2   Daughter

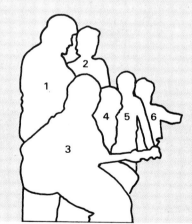

C

A family with adopted children
1   Mr Thomas
1   Mrs Thomas
3   Daughter Katie
4   Adopted daughter Sophie
5   Adopted son Matthew
6   Son Sam

D

An extended family
1   Grandmother
2   Mother Mrs Simms
3   Daughter Susan
4   Great Grandmother
5   Father Mr Simms

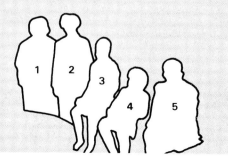

What is a family?

There are advantages and disadvantages to living in each of these family types. Think of some of these good and bad things now. Here are some clues to help you:

Would you like to live in a small family or a large family? Why?

Would you like to live with, near, or far away from other relatives like cousins, aunts and uncles or grandparents? Why?

Do you think large families need more or less help to deal with household jobs than small families? Why?

How many people are needed to make a family?

Must people have children to be a family?

Must people be married to be a family?

Must there always be a mother or father in a family?

So what is a family?

Draw a picture of your family. Write a few family notes about it like the ones on the page opposite.

People in families usually have certain jobs to do around the home. Make a table like these and show the jobs that go on in your house.

JOBS AT HOME	
WHO DOES IT?	THE JOBS
ME	wash up wipe up Make the beds Make coffee and tea Hoover Tidy Bedroom Shopping cleans the car
Mum	Wash up Cook Make the bed Hoover Shopping Make tea cuts the grass dusts
Dad	Decorates Wash up (sometimes) Wipe up (sometimes) Cuts the grass cleans the car
My Brothers and Sisters	Wash up wipe up Make the beds Make tea and coffee Hoover Tidy Bedroom Shopping cleans the car
Anybody Else (say who)	Tortise eats the grass (cuts)

JOBS AT HOME	
WHO DOES IT?	THE JOBS
ME	Wash up (Sometimes) Make bed. go Shopping (Sometimes) clean bedroom (Sometimes) feed the hamsters Make tea
Mum	wash clothes cooks decorates feeds dog hoover Makes tea and coffee Makes beds gardening
Dad	Decorates Washes car Washes up (sometimes) Makes tea and coffee Sits in chair and drinks tea with Paper
My Brothers and Sisters	Makes bed (Sometimes) goes Shopping makes tea and coffee feed the hamsters
Anybody Else (say who)	dog dusts

13

Family trees

History is about families because history is about people. Everybody is connected with someone else, sometimes closely like brothers and sisters, sometimes more distantly like second cousins. Sometimes these connections spread across long distances to different towns and sometimes to different countries. Sometimes members of one family do not even know each other. Other families all know each other very well.

These family connections also spread backwards through time, though most people do not know much about their own family history. But the fact that you are here now means that your *ancestors*, members of your family, were alive at the time of the Spanish Armada and the Roman invasion of Britain.

We can show how different people are related to each other in a single family by drawing a family tree. Here is part of a family tree. It shows just two *generations*, but it is possible to show many more.

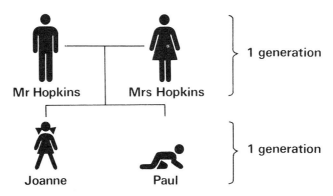

Instead of a drawing
a family tree can look
like this:

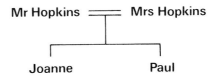

Here is a family tree with a third generation

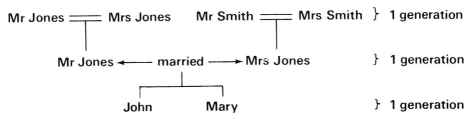

Now try to make a diagram of your family tree. Put in as many generations as you like. You may have to ask your family a few questions. This is the family tree of an Extended Family.

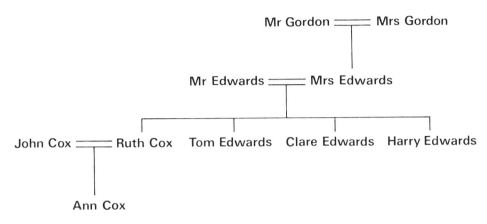

1. How many generations are shown?

2. How many grandchildren have Mr and Mrs Gordon?

3. Why doesn't Mrs Edwards have the same surname as her parents?

4. How many *descendants* have Mr and Mrs Edwards?

5. How many uncles has Ann Cox?

6. What relation is John Cox to Mr and Mrs Edwards?

7. What relation is Ann Cox to Mr and Mrs Gordon?

8. How many nieces are shown?

9. How many daughters have Mr and Mrs Edwards?

10. How many mothers are shown?

11. What relation is Harry Edwards to John Cox?

12. Who is Ann Cox's aunt?

13. What problems would you have if you were asked to draw a family tree like this for John Cox?

14. How may Ann Cox and Ruth Cox and John Cox appear on someone else's family tree?

Family trees can give us a lot of information.

Where families live

Some people have relatives who all live near each other. Other people have relatives who live in different parts of the country, and others have relatives who live in different parts of the world.

Here are three maps. The first shows a local area where a child and some of her relatives live. The second is a map of Britain and shows how two children's relatives are scattered across it. The third map shows the world and the countries where these children's relatives live.

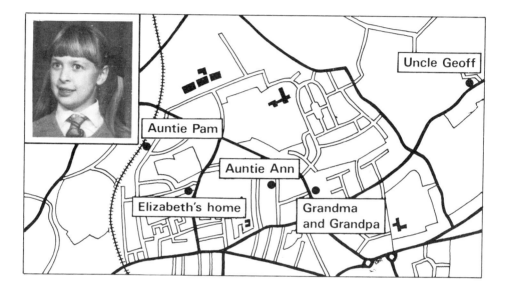

Write down the answers to as many of these questions as you can. If none of your relatives lives in another country, for example, you will not be able to answer question 5.

1. How can relatives help each other?

2. How can relatives help each other when they live long distances apart?

3. When relatives live a long way from each other, how do they keep in contact?

4. Make a list of relatives who do not live in your town. Alongside each write the name of their town.

5. Make a list of relatives who live in other countries. Alongside each write the name of their country.

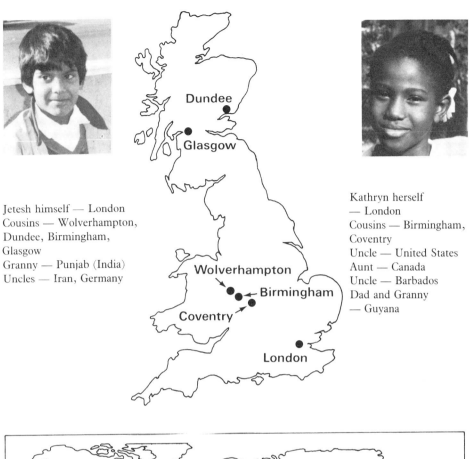

Jetesh himself — London
Cousins — Wolverhampton,
Dundee, Birmingham,
Glasgow
Granny — Punjab (India)
Uncles — Iran, Germany

Kathryn herself
— London
Cousins — Birmingham,
Coventry
Uncle — United States
Aunt — Canada
Uncle — Barbados
Dad and Granny
— Guyana

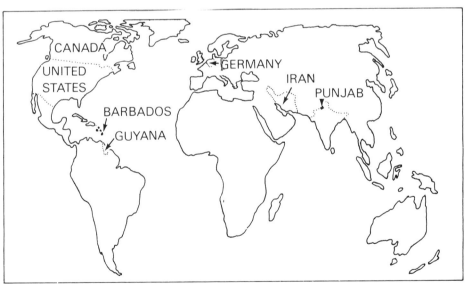

6. Make a list of relatives you know well, and another list of
   relatives whom you do not know very well. Why do you think
   you have two separate groups of relatives?

17

Memories

Remembering your own life

It is fairly easy to remember things which interest you. For example, if you enjoy football you can probably remember the names of your school team or your local team. As this book is about you, we are going to find out what you can remember about yourself.

Can you remember the date on which you were born? You might even know which day of the week it was. But can you remember what the weather was like on that day, or what was on television, or what the family had for tea? No, of course not.

So what is the first thing you can remember? Some hazy picture in your mind, perhaps of a place or a person? Often this first memory is jogged by something that someone says, or a photograph, or a similar event happening again, or even a faint, familiar smell. Everybody has a first memory, but everybody has a different one.

Memory-joggers

Here are some ideas which may help to jog your memory about your early life. Read through them first and think of a few more which might be helpful.

1. If you went to a nursery school or playgroup, what can you remember about it — the building, the toys and games, the grown-ups and the children?

2. What is your oldest toy? How old is it? When did you get it? What was your favourite toy before you started school?

3. Try making a list of all the places where you have been.

4. What has been your best holiday or best day out?

5. Have you always lived in the same house or town? Where else have you lived?

6. Can you remember your first day at school?

7. Can you remember your first teacher?

8. Can you remember who was in your first class and whom you played with?

9. Can you remember being in a ceremony like a wedding? Describe it. Who else was there?

10. What events can you remember seeing on television or in the newspapers?

Sources

Make a list of *sources* which may help us to discover what happened to us in the time which we cannot remember.

People as observers

Writing from memory

Read these two reports, which children wrote about their teacher. Examine each one carefully and notice where they are the same and where they are different.

Is it possible to draw a portrait of this teacher from the information you are given by the two children?

How can the reports be different when the children are writing about a person they know so well — their class teacher? These reports were made for homework when the children had only their memories to rely on. It is not easy to make a good description. It is hard to guess weight and height and remember a hair colour and style exactly.

See what you can do

Choose someone who is not in your classroom and describe them. It could be another teacher, for example. Imagine you are a detective writing about a criminal so that other people can recognise him or her.

You will find that it is easy to forget quite important details, so before you start to write decide what things are needed for a really good description. Here are some to start you off:

height
hair colour
eye colour

Report One

He is aged about 35-40. He is about 5 ft 9 inches tall and weighs about 11 stone. He has light brown hair. He has a round face which has two moles on it, one on his cheek and one above his eyebrow He has a round chin and a high forehead. I think he has hazel eyes and he also has quite bushy eyebrows. Yesturday he was wearing some dark blue trousers, a light blue jumper and some smart black shoes. I think he usually dresses quite nicely.

Report Two

This person has brown hair with bits of grey around his ears. He weighs about thirteen stone and he has blue eyes. He is about five foot four in height and takes about size eight in shoe size. His hair is wavy and is slightly flicked on the left hand side. He is wearing a blue cardigan and blue trousers with a brown jacket. He wears a tie to match and looks very smart. He has a round chin and wears a ring on each finger. He wears brown shoes and has a big brown bag His age is about 45.

Opinions

Different points of view

Lots of people know you. There are people at home, for example, and many of the people in your street and at your local shops. If you belong to a club many of the people there will recognise you and many of them will have some opinion about you, even if they have never even spoken to you. Some of their opinions may not be very nice.

Let's look at opinions more closely by investigating what a family thought someone was like as a baby.

Asking questions is easy. It is sorting out the answers that presents the problem. If you ask different people the same question you may receive a new answer each time you ask. People have their own opinions because they see things in different ways.

Here are some reasons for the opinions given here:

Grandma Only saw the baby when she was expected and it was washed and tidy.

Dad Can remember the many times he had to get up in the night because the baby was crying and is glad that time is over.

Mum Was very proud of the baby. Remembers that it was difficult to feed and has often laughed about that since because the child now eats everything it is offered.

Big sister Was very upset when the toy was spoilt and still remembers even though it was a good many years ago.

As good historical detectives it is our job to find out not only what opinions are but also the reasons for those opinions.

People and questions

Make a list of people who might know something about you when you were very small. Alongside each one put a star if they knew you well, two stars if they knew you very well.

Now make a list of things you would like to know about yourself. For example, 'When did I cut my first teeth?' Here are some clues which might help:

teeth
sleep
nappies
walk
talk
toys
hospital

If you can, ask each person in your list the same questions about yourself and write down their replies.

Bias

Unfair statements

Look back at the two reports by the children who described their teacher. Is there enough information for you to want to be in this teacher's class? What else would you want to know about him?

Saying what a person looks like gives a very limited description. People may be beautiful but mean. They may look bad-tempered but may really be kind and good-natured. Before forming opinions about someone we need to know something about that person's *personality*.

Here are four faces. On the next page are fifty adjectives. Choose adjectives which you think are right for each face. You may choose as many adjectives as you wish for each face, but they must fit with one another. For example, a face may not be described as cruel *and* kind.

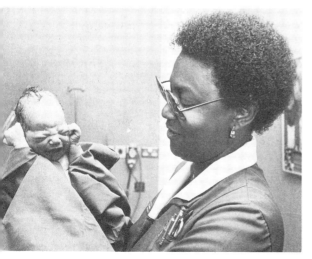

kind	excitable	bad-tempered
helpful	gentle	shy
calm	mean	happy
fierce	dishonest	patient
generous	lazy	sociable
honest	nice	sensible
hardworking	big-headed	easy-going
horrible	relaxed	quiet
modest	rude	stupid
stubborn	unpopular	pompous
polite	weak	pleasant
popular	poor	confident
powerful	friendly	miserable
rich	strict	impatient
snobbish	selfish	unfriendly
inconsiderate	clever	silly
unhelpful	funny	

That exercise was not very fair. It was asking you to jump to *conclusions*. You have no way of knowing what these people are really like. The adjectives do not describe their appearance but suggest what their characters are like.

You have no way of knowing whether the tramp is an actor in disguise, or the nurse is really a burglar, or that kind old lady is a bank-robber, or the business man is really a murderer. You already have opinions about tramps, nurses, business men and little old ladies and you used these opinions in this exercise.

Your opinions showed *bias*. They caused you to make quick but unfair conclusions.

Of the four characters shown on page 22, who was the most biased in their judgement? (Think hard. This is a difficult question.)

Can you think of anyone who is biased towards you? Against you? Are you biased towards someone? Against someone?

Photographic evidence

Using photographs as clues

Changes are taking place all the time in ourselves and in the world around us. One of the best ways to see these changes is to look at photographs.

Look at the photograph of my ancestors below. If it were taken today, what would be different about it?

Photographs may show how people change as they grow older, and how fashions in clothes change. They may show changes caused by building and demolition, and in the way people enjoy themselves.

You can discover many interesting facts from photographs. It is important to look not just at the main subject but also at the background. This might give clues about where and when the photograph was taken and who else was there. Clues may also be found on the backs of photographs, where a date, a name and a place may have been recorded.

Photographs may also show similarities and differences. For example, no doubt somebody in your family has compared the way you look with the looks of someone else. Here is a photograph of me, my wife and our three children, Elizabeth, Matthew and Christopher. Look closely. Do any of the children look like their parents or their ancestors?

Who do you look like? Who do your brothers, sisters and cousins look like? Who do your parents look like?

Chronological order

Put these photographs of Elizabeth in order of age. We call this *chronological order*. Start with the earliest photograph of Elizabeth. Try to *estimate* (or guess) how old she was in each photograph. Say what evidence caused you to make your guess.

You should be able to work out a good many things by looking closely at these pictures. For example:

1. Where was A taken?

2. Where was D taken?

3. Who are the other people in B?

4. What might have been the occasion when Elizabeth had her photograph taken in F?

5. Which photographs were taken when the weather was warm?

6. Elizabeth is 8. How has she changed in the last 8 years?

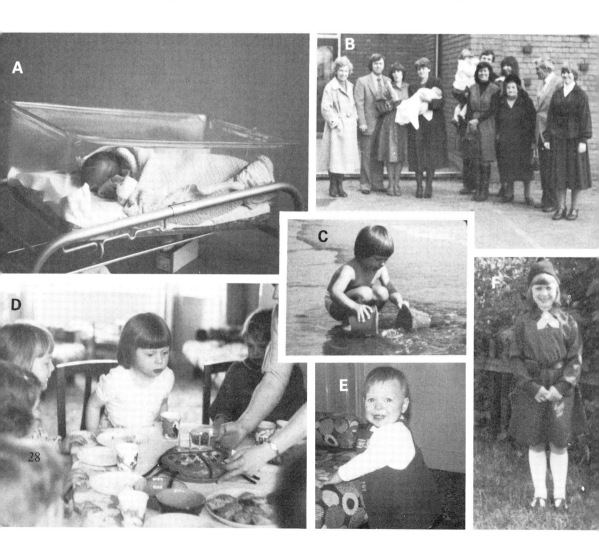

28

Memorable occasions

All through our lives we take part in memorable occasions. Some happen regularly like birthdays; others are more special like weddings and first days at school. Many events are recorded on photographs and form a visual diary of our lives. The photographs on this page show some special occasions. What event is shown in each photograph?

Make two lists: (a) some special occasions in your life
(b) regular occasions on which you were photographed.

29

Summarising

Summarising time

A photograph captures a moment in time. But history is more than any one moment. However, if we recorded every tiny detail it would take a lifetime to write it all down. So we must *summarise*.

Yesterday

Look at what three children wrote about 'yesterday'. Remember that all these children were in the same class and their accounts are all about the same day. Examine each one carefully and note where the children's information is the same. Are there any facts which are only mentioned by one child?

Why are the accounts different? How many reasons can you think of?

These accounts are different in ways that written or spoken reports often are different. What is important to one person may not be quite so important to another. The children who wrote accounts of yesterday had to summarise a much longer piece of writing with the same title. They had to write a passage of a certain length, making decisions about what to put in and what to leave out.

> Yesterday I went swimming at Crown pools. I went for my bronze. We had to do a dive and then swim five yards. and then do a duck dive. The We swam two lengths, After that we swam under water. The last thing to do was a Straddle. Jump. Then we all climbed out, and got changed and went back to School and listened to PoP music.

Porridge Eggs
n, Lunch Sausages
Rice Pudding.
ans on Toast,
Chocolate
milk Drink.

It was 17th of October and I woke up had breakfast got to School I done some work and then went Swimming. We go every wednesday. Then it was dinner after my dinner it was the afternoon we done art. Then it was home time. After School I went to Sigate with the Six a side football team with the School, We come first. I went home had my tea and went to bed.

On wednesday 17th October I walked to School and went in to Hymn practise. Then we did math for about ½ hour. At 10.45 we went Swimming and I demonstrated to Mr Kendals group frount crawl. When we were dressed and back at school. We had dinner. Then we went out to Rugby touch. In the afternoon we had art and we drew a tree with pastals. Then we went out to play. At 3.00pm we listened to a tape pop music from 1950's – 1984.

Now it's your turn. First write as much as you can remember about yesterday. (If today is Monday, then write about last Friday.) When you have finished shorten your report to about 70 words. Compare your summary with those of other people in your class. Notice how some of the things which you thought were important did not matter at all to them.

Yesterday's news

National newspapers

The most recent history books are newspapers. What happened yesterday is now history. We have a record of what happened yesterday in yesterday's newspapers. But is that record reliable? A newspaper is only a summary of a day's news. You have already found that what is important to one person may not be so important to another. An article in a newspaper is just one account of what happened; a different reporter might tell the same story differently.

Look at the front pages of the three daily newspapers shown here. These are all from national newspapers published on the same day.

1. What is the main story for each newspaper?

2. Is more space given to a picture or to the written story?

Look through different national newspapers which are all for the same day. Choose one event which was reported in all of them and compare what different papers said about it. Notice:

1. How much space the event was given

2. Whereabouts in the paper the report came

3. How big the title was

4. Whether there was a photograph to accompany the report.

Selling newspapers

It is important to remember that a journalist must not write too much. There are many news items competing for space in the paper. The journalist or his editor have to make decisions about what to keep in and what to leave out. Journalists and television news editors do this all the time, so that sometimes they do not give a true impression of what really happened. Remember too that editors want people to buy their papers. People find some news items more interesting than others.

Local newspapers

Now here are two local evening papers published on the day before the national papers on pages 32–3. What are their main stories? Why do you think they are different from the main story in the national newspapers?

Here is a clue:

Many people read a national newspaper and nearly everybody sees television news.

Note: The air crash took place on the night of August 11, too late to be reported in morning papers of August 12.

Change

The speed of change

Everybody has changed since they were born. Your neighbourhood has changed; your town has changed; the world has changed.

Look at these three pictures of a boy who was born in 1970. He is shown at three ages. In what ways is the life of this boy different at each age?

1 year   7 years   15 years

Think of: clothes, hobbies, pastimes, food. Any more?

What events might have happened in the life of this boy by each age shown? Who or what might help you to find out?

Being an historical detective often means looking for evidence of change. Things change at different speeds. Some things change in minutes; other things take long periods of time to change.

A. What has changed within the last few minutes? What might have happened?

B. Some changes are seasonal. What change has happened here within the last few months?

C. How has this car changed since it was made?

D. What sort of building might this have once been? In what ways has it changed? Imagine some of the things which have happened to this building.

A. Some changes take place in minutes. Can you think of any other examples? Think of food, for example.

B. Some changes take place over months.
Can you think of any examples? Think of animals and plants.

C. Some changes take years to happen. Think of more examples.

D. Some changes take place over hundreds of years.
Think of more examples.

Documentary or written evidence

Evidence of you

Suppose an alien spacecraft flew over one day and made you vanish. What evidence would there be that you had actually lived at all? A lot! People would have known you. Your home and school would have many pieces of evidence. There would be your toys, your books. Cupboards would contain your clothes. There might be lots of photographs.

What evidence can you find of your life? Do you have any certificates which might show your hobbies or any clubs or organisations to which you belong?

Can you find any other *documentary or written* evidence such as letters, birthday cards, savings books, appointment cards or newspaper cuttings?

Why do people keep such things for long periods of time? Do some seem more important than others?

Look at some of the evidence for Elizabeth's life on the next page. Which piece of evidence shows that Elizabeth was actually born?

What tells you something about her family?

Is there anything to show what she likes doing in her spare time?

Decide which pieces of evidence Elizabeth might *need* to keep for the rest of her life.

Certificate of Birth

No fee is chargeable for this certificate

GG 135668

1 & 2 ELIZ. 2 CH. 20

CERTIFICATE   OF BIRTH

Name and Surname   Elizabeth Louise COCKCROFT

Sex   Female

Date of Birth   Fifteenth April 1977

Place of Birth
Registration District   Leeds
Sub-district   Leeds

I, GEORGE BRABBS   Registrar of Births and Deaths for the sub-district of   LEEDS   in the Registration District of   do hereby certify that the above particulars have been compiled from an entry in a register in my custody.

Date - 4 MAY 1977

CSENK/28

G. Brabbs.
Registrar of Births and Deaths.

CAUTION:—Any person who (1) falsifies any of the particulars on this certificate, or (2) uses a falsified certificate as true, knowing it to be false, is liable to prosecution.

Now we're the
HAPPIEST FAMILY!

NAME Elizabeth Louise

DATE 15th April 1977

WEIGHT 7lbs 1oz

PARENTS Frances + John

Mr. NICHOLAS MANN, B.D.S.
Dental Surgeon

'STAFFA LODGE'
326 NORWICH ROAD,
IPSWICH.
IP1 4HD.

Telephone: Ispwich 41720.

Matthew + Elizabeth

Your next appointment is
TUES 15TH   Oct 4:40

A fee may be charged if an appointment is broken or cancelled without 24 hours' notice Please bring this card with you

---

Constable ....DISTRICT

16th Ipswich ....COMPANY/PACK
(Name and Number)

BADGE CERTIFICATE

Interest Badge

I/we have tested   Elizabeth Cockcroft

for   Book Lovers   Interest Badge. She has reached a high personal standard and I/we recommend that the badge is awarded.

Service Badge

I/we hereby certify that

has reached the required standard for

Service Badge and recommend that the badge is awarded.

Signed: *J. Finain*   Testers

Remarks: Date 14th February 1985

MISS E L COCKCROFT

Midland Bank plc
41 WOODBRIDGE ROAD EAST
IPSWICH SUFFOLK IP4 5QN

GRIFFIN SAVERS ACCOUNT
Statement of Deposit Account
SUBJECT TO NOTICE OF WITHDRAWAL AS NOTIFIED

1984 Sheet 1 Account No. 23013138	DEBIT	CREDIT	BALANCE Credit C Debit D
OCT23 SUNDRIES		10.00	10.00 C
OCT23 BALANCE CARRIED FORWARD			10.00 C

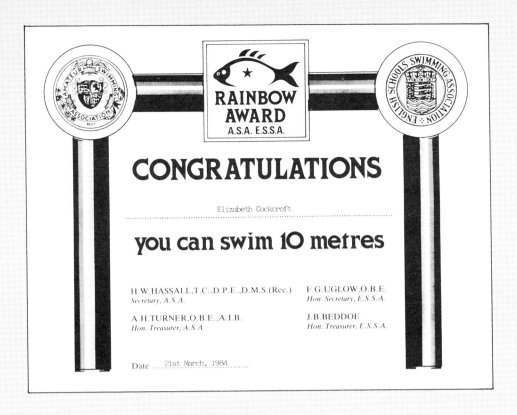

Certificate: RAINBOW AWARD A.S.A. E.S.S.A.

CONGRATULATIONS

Elizabeth Cockcroft

you can swim 10 metres

H.W.HASSALL,T.C.,D.P.E.,D.M.S.(Rec.)
Secretary, A.S.A.

F.G.UGLOW,O.B.E.
Hon. Secretary, E.S.S.A.

A.H.TURNER,O.B.E.,A.I.B.
Hon. Treasurer, A.S.A.

J.B.BEDDOE
Hon. Treasurer, E.S.S.A.

Date ...... 21st March, 1984 ....

Evidence at school

Most of your life so far has been shared between home and school. You have some ideas about how to trace your history at home. Now we shall try to trace it at school.

1. What evidence have you got about the work you have done and what adults thought about it?

2. Have you taken part in any sports events? Are there any certificates to show that you did?

3. What evidence have you got about school trips or school concerts? Is there anything to show that you took part?

4. Have you got a Parent-Teacher Association at your school?

5. How does your school raise money?

6. What sort of things have your parents or teachers been involved in to raise money for the school? Did you take part too?

Look at the documentary evidence on these pages. Which pieces are connected with work inside the classroom and which with school life outside?

Name: School work   Date:

MYSTERY PERSON

Ideas	Evidence for Ideas
1 Banks with Midland bank	Letter from bank
2. His names Peter	letter from James Nash
3. Last name is Fisher	Same letter
4. Teacher	Nut book
5. Address is 11 Ransome close	letter from Marion Casey
6. Has moved house	
7. Ran the Ipswich Marathon	Vehicle Document
8 Has a wife	medal
9 Has a child	Photo
10 Has a Fiat	Photo
11 Wrote a book	Keys
12 Works at Northgate school	Book cover
13 Might be going abroad	Travel slip leflet

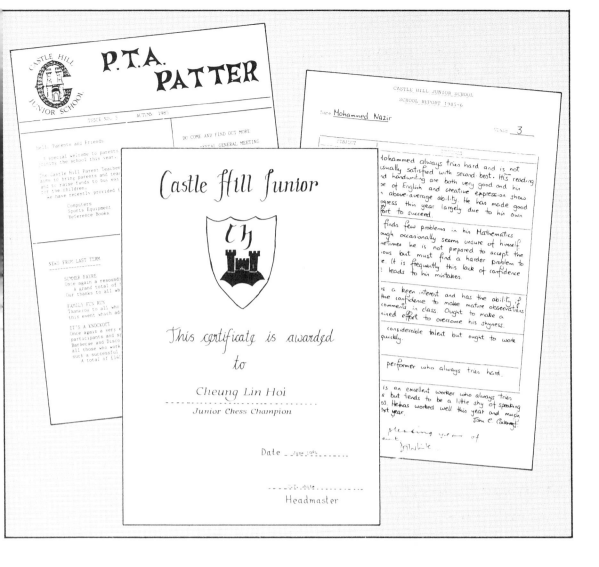

Try to find evidence like the illustrations here and make a history of life at your school. Decide how far to go back. It might be for just one year or for one term or for several years. Make the dates as accurate as possible and put all the documents in *chronological* (date) order.

Newspaper research

The local paper might have published articles about some of your school events — sports' days or summer fairs, for example. The newspaper office should have back numbers of the paper. Ask if you can see them. You might find that parents or teachers have kept newspaper cuttings of important events in the life of the school.

41

A historical detective story

The need for more evidence

Read this article from a newspaper. It is a true story which happened in May 1985. Suppose you were a historian who found the article hundreds of years later. What could you find out from it? Remember that you have *only* the article to go on. See if you can answer these questions.

1. What did the attacker look like?

2. How many people saw the attack?

3. Why do you think the description of the attacker is so brief?

4. Make a sketch of the attacker. What facts are missing about his appearance?

5. If you did not know what jeans were, would you be able to tell from this article? What about the rest of the clothes?

6. How many reporters worked on the story?

7. Would you be able to tell from the article what pensioners are?

8. Do you think both men and women were members of the club? How can you tell?

9. Could you tell what 'glue sniffing' means?

10. How could you find out where Tacket Street was? What does the article tell you about it?

BATTLING OLD FOLKS

Brave ladies send attacker packing

A STICK-WIELDING attacker was sent packing by two brave old ladies after a terrifying assault at an Ipswich pensioners' meeting.

The man burst into the town centre meeting brandishing a three-foot long stick and demanded money from the frightened women, aged between 65 and 90.

When they refused, the attacker — thought to have been glue sniffing just before the frightening incident — lashed out with the weapon, landing a painful blow on one woman.

But then the man was chased out by two brave members of the Shaftesbury Club — even

By TERRY HUNT and PAUL BROWES

though they came under attack themselves.

"Under the circumstances it was a very courageous thing to do," said Det. Ch. Insp. John Ingle, the man leading the probe into the frightening daylight attack.

"They persuaded the man to leave the building although he was hitting them with the piece of wood as well," said Mr. Ingle.

The attack came as members of the club were enjoying their regular meeting at the United Reformed Church in Tacket Street, yesterday afternoon.

"He just went into the room carrying a three-foot long piece of wood and demanded money from them. When they refused he hit one lady across the shoulder. Fortunately she was not seriously hurt," said Mr. Ingle.

"It was then that two other club members, both of them elderly ladies, managed to persuade him to leave. They then called us, but despite extensive efforts on our behalf he had disappeared."

Mr. Ingle said the stick-wielding attacker was aged 18-20, of thin build, wearing jeans and a beige and blue speckled crew neck top. Police also believe he may have been sniffing glue before the assault.

"This happened in broad daylight and we believe there is a good chance that someone saw this man with the stick. If anyone can help us, we would be glad to hear from them on Ipswich 55811," said Mr. Ingle.

43

In my time

There are four and a half thousand million people in the world. That means there are four and a half thousand million people with personal histories. All these people have different stories to tell, different memories, different ideas of what happened to them and why things happened. Some people are involved in world events like wars, strikes, floods or hurricanes. Some people have happy memories, some sad.

Making a retrograph

If you look at the graph you can see how some world events have overlapped with the lives of my family. This is called a *retrograph*. You can make your own, about your own life, putting in world events if you like. I have chosen things which interest me, but your ideas may be quite different. I have stopped at 1986, but by the time you read this we shall be further on in time, so you can put in more dates.

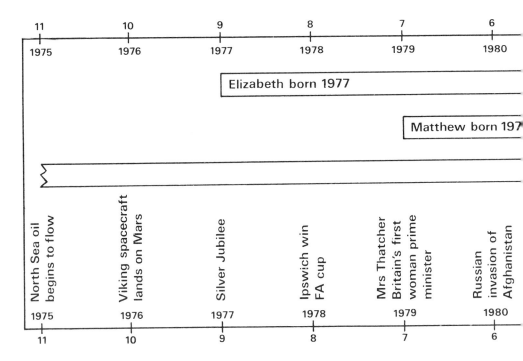

Look closely at the example. You will need some squared paper.

Decide how many years you want your retrograph to go back through time. Mark a time line on your paper, starting on the right-hand side and going to the left. Mark in the years and how many years ago each year is from now.

Pick a subject (you?) whose time-span you want to show. Mark it as a line moving from left to right. Almost anything which lasts for a span of time — toys, pets, for example — can be included.

Pick events which happened at a certain time. Write them across your graph at the correct date — Royal Wedding, for example. Events which happen at the same time are said to be *contemporary*.

Mark other time spans and events on your graph, but do not make it too crowded. Give your retrograph a suitable title.

By the way . . .

In the time it took you to read this page thousands of people have been born and thousands have died.

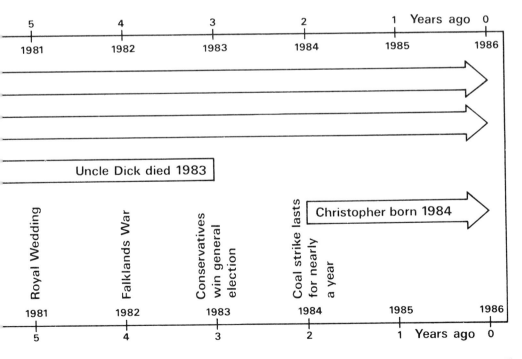

A time capsule

Capturing time gone by

As you worked through this book you should have found out a great deal about yourself. So you could write your *autobiography*. Instead of doing that, you could collect evidence about yourself and make your own museum. Or, like a pirate on a desert island, you could bury or hide away some of your personal belongings in a time capsule. Be careful though that things you put in it will not be needed in the future. Ask your teacher about the things you want to include.

Everyday things are very important, even if we take them for granted. People in the future may find them more interesting than we do.

The children in these photographs buried a time capsule about life in 1985. Their lists of what was important included all sorts of clothes, household items, kitchen packets and many other things. What would you include?

On the other hand, perhaps your time capsule may be just a box of personal belongings about the span of your life so far. Do not forget where you have put it!

EADT in school's 'life in '85' time capsule

A TIME capsule containing items depicting life in 1985, including a copy of the EADT, was buried at an East Anglian primary school yesterday.

It was buried by pupils at Castle Hill Junior School, Ipswich, who have contributed more than 400 items.

These include items such as a computer game, video tape and a tacograph.

Deputy headmaster Mr. John Cockcroft said that as well as portraying life in 1985, the venture was an exercise in classification.

A plaque provided by the school's Parent Teacher Association will be screwed onto a paving slab covering the four foot deep hole.

Mr. Cockcroft said it had not been decided in which year the capsule would be opened.

"It will be opened when people's curiosity gets the better of them," he explained.

Somebody else's treasure

This is thought to have been buried at the time of the Great Fire of London over 300 years ago. Why should anyone have wanted to bury it?

Index

ancestors 14
autobiography 46

bias 24, 25

change 26, 27, 35, 36
chronological order 28, 41
clues 7, 8, 9, 10, 26–7
conclusions, jumping to 25
contemporary 45

descendants 15
detective 20, 23, 42–3
documents 37

evidence 7, 9, 10, 26, 37–41
experts 3, 22–3

families 11–15, 17, 26, 27
family tree 14, 15

generation 14

memories 18
memory-joggers 19
museum 46

newspapers 32–34, 42

observers, people as 20–21
occasions 29
opinions 22, 24, 25

personality 5, 24
photographs 18, 26, 27, 30, 37, 46

questionnaire 4–6
questions 3–5, 22–3

rank 7, 8
relatives 13, 14, 15, 16, 17
replicas 10
retrograph 44, 45

source 3, 19
statements 24
summarising 30, 31

time capsule 46, 47
treasure 47

unfair statements 24

written evidence 37